IMAGES
of America

PROVO

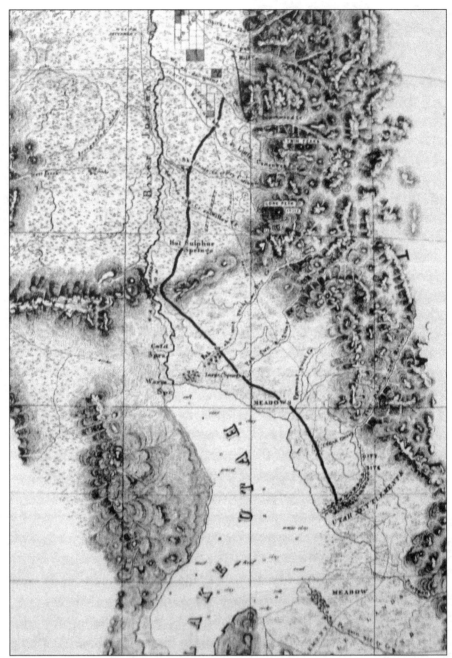

In 1849–1950, Col. J.J. Ebert, the chief of the US Topographical Bureau, sent Capt. Howard Stansbury and his group to survey the "Wild West." J.W. Gunnison and Charles Preuss drew this map of the mountains, valleys, and deserts. If travelers wanted to go further than the Mormon settlements, they faced a hostile desert. But in the valley, as John C. Fremont wrote on his expedition of 1845, "the lake is bordered by a plain, where the soil is generally good. . . . This would be an excellent locality for stock farms." (BYU Collection.)

ON THE COVER: This horse show took place on the lot where the City and County Building now stands. (L. Perry Collection, BYU Library.)

IMAGES
of America
PROVO

Marilyn Brown and Valerie Holladay

ARCADIA
PUBLISHING

Published by Arcadia Publishing
Charleston, South Carolina

Library of Congress Control Number: 2011920842

For all general information, please contact Arcadia Publishing:
Telephone 843-853-2070
Fax 843-853-0044
E-mail sales@arcadiapublishing.com
For customer service and orders:
Toll-Free 1-888-313-2665

Visit us on the Internet at www.arcadiapublishing.com

For the dedicated Utah County historian D. Robert Carter.

CONTENTS

Acknowledgments   6

Introduction   7

1.   Refuge   9

2.   Thriving through Famine and War   21

3.   Building Industry   43

4.   Community Services   65

5.   Enriching Lives   81

6.   Up-to-Date City   109

ACKNOWLEDGMENTS

When Valerie Holladay—who knew of my *Provo: A Story of People in Motion*, which was published with John C. Moffitt in 1974—asked me if I might want to help with another book on Provo, I hesitated. Thirty-five years ago, pictures were hard to come by. One family agreed to bring their scrapbook to the Brigham Young University (BYU) Photo Studio while the professionals photographed it. They did not let it out of their sight. Now that those photographs and many others are safe in the archives of BYU and available online, the task is not quite as impossible. We owe Tom Wells, curator at the L. Tom Perry Special Collections, a great debt of gratitude for allowing us to use these wonderful images. The *Daily Herald* and the LDS Church Library were also helpful.

For photographs of present-day monuments and events, digital photography has made our task much easier. Hiking to the Spanish Fork cross, we got a good picture of the spot where Silvestre Velez de Escalante and Francisco Atanasio Dominguez looked out over the Utah Valley in 1776. After taking a shot of the cross, we tramped through the dry grass to look west toward the direction they took after they had befriended the Ute Indians and promised them they would return.

Though the Spaniards did not come back, many other explorers and trappers came to hunt and fish this pristine country. The best records of this early time have been gathered together by conscientious local historian D. Robert Carter, who was willing to share his comprehensive work and look over the final draft. Roosevelt's Work Projects Administration generated a great deal of material, and other authors, such as John C. Moffitt, J. Marinus Jensen, and Kenneth L. Cannon II, have helped fill in some of the details. The final product must be attributed to the expertise of Arcadia Publishing and the patience of Jared Jackson, Crystal Conklin, Stacia Bannerman, and Kristie Kelly.

INTRODUCTION

Once, a large area in Utah, Nevada, and Idaho was covered by Lake Bonneville. To this day, hikers in the highest mountains still come upon small snail and conch shells winking from the pine needles like savvy eyes that have seen our ancient history across thousands and thousands of years. As the water receded, after the time of the dinosaurs and Paleolithic people, it dried up into a string of puddles that still exist today as the Great Salt Lake, Utah Lake, and others.

The archaic cultures lived on what game they could extract from their surroundings—fish, birds, and deer. Immigrant groups such as the Fremont Indians began to farm, as well as hunt and fish, around the freshwater lakes, but they left the hostile salty desert lake alone. About 900 AD, a new group of nomadic people came. The new Indians near Utah Lake became the Timpanogots Utes. A rough translation of *Timpanogots* is "people who live near the mouth of a rocky canyon through which water flows."

The discovery of these Timpanogots Utes and other natives in 1776 by Francisco Atanasio Dominguez and Silvestre Velez de Escalante, two Spanish Franciscan explorers looking for a route from Santa Fe to California, resulted in the first written record of the area. It is believed these Christian missionaries stopped on a knoll just south of Spanish Fork and not only left their Spanish legacy in the name of the city and the "Old Spanish Trail" but also promised they would return to bring their religion to the pleasant people they found inhabiting the "Valley of Our Lady of Mercy of Timpanogos."

Though Dominguez and Escalante never returned to Utah Valley, their maps and journals excited hundreds of Spanish explorers, trappers, and miners to make their way west to "New Spain." An ambitious interpreter by the name of Manuel Mestas, who worked with the Utes for 50 years to secure peace, noted that when he first came, these people were without horses. The entry of horses to their culture changed their way of life. They began stealing the animals from the Spanish, and Mestas was forced to interfere.

With horses, the Utes became warlike and began to implement slave trading—kidnapping and selling human beings to get more horses, guns, and ammunition. Many Christian Spaniards were appalled at the practice of slave-trading, but from 1800 to 1847, they found that if they refused to cooperate, the Utes became angry and sometimes went on killing sprees. After such slaughters, the frightened Spaniards felt fortunate to steal away with their lives.

In the 1820s, British, French-Canadian, and American trappers risked their lives to harvest furs in Utah Valley—especially beaver pelts for the popular high-topped beaver hats. The trappers often staked claims to certain areas that acquired their names.

In 1824, the famous French trapper Etienne Proveau hunted near the mouth of a river later named the Provo River. The story of Proveau's escape from one killing spree is a riveting tale of horror. When he and his group offered to smoke the peace pipe with a group, they shed their weapons to appease the Shoshones, but many were soon slaughtered in an ugly massacre. Records vary on who escaped, but Etienne Proveau, a hefty man of around 300 pounds, was one of the few who got away.

Other explorers came. In 1826, armed with gifts of red ribbon, razors, knives, and tobacco, Jedediah Strong Smith made a treaty with the Utes that trappers could hunt unmolested, though the agreement did not last. In 1827, Daniel T. Potts left the following apt description of this rich valley: "This is a most beautiful country. It is intersected by a number of transparent streams. The grass is at this time from six to twelve inches in height, and in full bloom. The snow that falls seldom remains more than a week." And finally, John C. Fremont, the "Great Pathfinder," published such winsome details that his writing influenced the Mormon immigrants to make this lush area their home.

When Brigham Young met with Jim Bridger in the summer of 1847, the famous scout discouraged the leader from taking his people directly into the territory of the hostile Utes or to the Shoshones to the north, near Ogden's Hole. So on July 24, the Mormons settled in a country no one wanted—near the basin where the freshwater mountain streams converged and putrefied—the Great Salt Lake.

But the Mormons found more food for their cattle in the greener valley to the south and also good fishing in Utah Lake. Most of the time they got along with the Indians, until a group of native thieves began stealing the cattle. A settlers' posse came down to stop this practice, killing the men and taking the women and children back to Salt Lake City. Brigham Young agreed that 33 families should go to Utah Valley to "civilize the Indians" and plant crops. This group, stopping at French trapper Etienne Proveau's "hole," became the first settlement south of Salt Lake Valley, Provo.

Not only Indian troubles escalated. Eight years later, when the US Army came to quell the "Mormon rebellion," Salt Lake City residents filled their houses with straw, left someone there to light it, and came down to camp in the streets of Provo. Though the danger passed when the army moved out to Camp Floyd, located west of Utah Lake, there were still risks from the presence of worldly soldiers who came into town to drink and carouse.

Provo's industry began to thrive from trading with the Army and with travelers on the trails. After the golden spike was driven in 1869, Provo was accessible by rail and alive with blacksmith shops, dry goods, and eventually a streetcar, which took pleasure-seekers out to swim and picnic at the lake or south to the hot springs in Spanish Fork Canyon.

Because of Mormon polygamy, practiced in Provo and all along the Wasatch bench, the new state of Deseret could not seat its senate candidates. Even monogamist Reed Smoot had a difficult time being accepted. It was 1896 before Utah achieved statehood. When it did happen, many fine people took the reins in Provo. Brigham Young University educated them for leadership. Technical education began with what later became Utah Valley University. Provo entered the 20th century with solid industries and banks, machine shops, and superb woolen mills that offered many jobs.

Provo's woolen mill manufactured clothing and blankets for America's soldiers involved in World War I, and the steel mill contributed metal for the war effort during World War II. When the Depression came, Provo supported the WPA. Soon, hospitals and schools proliferated along with clinics and other health industries, such as NuSkin, Nature's Sunshine, and Neways. Provo's intellectual prowess also generated computer industries, like Novell, Word Perfect, and others.

Today's award for America's "Least Stressful City" is an accomplishment Provo looks on with pride. Clean streets, lovely homes, and successful businesses surround the County Building and the central park where the old Mormon Tabernacle graces a peaceful square. Visitors at the new Health and Justice Building, the Covey Center, or BYU can see artwork displayed or attend artistic events. The new convention center near the Marriott Hotel has planned to keep the old Taylor Buildings and other historical treasures intact. Provo is a comfortable place to live and work, a place that has come a long way from its colorful past.

Unless otherwise marked, all images in the book came from BYU.edu/library, Digital Collections, and Photographs.

One

REFUGE

To the immigrants who populated Utah Valley, the Wasatch Mountains were more than just spectacular scenery. Like these fences, built later, the hills were a barrier that furnished some protection from those who persecuted others for their religious beliefs. Nestled close to this buffer, they felt safe to explore further, move out from Salt Lake, and risk their lives to make peace with the native populations in order to found new cities. One of the first was Provo.

Entering this amazing valley in late March 1849, the weary settlers would have found the bodies of water lying before them as pristine and beautiful as this empty scene behind Timpanogos Mountain. The stark drama of this image emphasizes how the puddles of Bonneville may have looked for centuries before the Europeans arrived. For thousands of years before the settlers put down roots, Native American cultures roamed the luxuriant land and fished the remaining waters of the dwindling Lake Bonneville. When Utah Lake's waters periodically recede, bones of these ancient inhabitants emerge from the mud.

11

The first record of a European visit to Utah Valley was made in 1776 by Fathers Dominguez and Escalante, who left not only the "Spanish" in Spanish Fork and the Old Spanish Trail but also glowing reports of Utah Valley—"the beauty of the streams . . . the cool nights and pleasant days." Modern Catholics constructed this cross on the foothills where these fathers might have stood. (Marilyn Brown.)

This image of Utah Lake, as it looks in 2010, suggests that what Escalante and Dominguez saw was a great fertile basin where the possibility for civilization sparked their imaginations. They wrote how they wanted to build series of villages in this valley, but it was close to a century before that dream began to materialize under the leadership of Brigham Young. (Marilyn Brown.)

On their trek to find a safe trail to Monterey, California, the Spanish fathers were in Colorado on the Gunnison River when they met a friendly visiting Ute and his son, who both might have looked much like this man. The Indian offered to take the explorers to his home in "Yuta." Growing attached to his traveling companions, the Ute guide took Escalante's first name, Silvestre, and shed tears when the friars left. Although the explorers promised to come the following year and establish the Christian religion, it did not happen.

On the next wave of travelers were the trappers. In 1824, French explorer Etienne Proveau caught beavers, bear, and cougars near his hole. He had no idea that a city would be named after the river he frequented or that this community would eventually rise like a star on the American scene, named by the Sperling List in 2004 the "least stressful" mid-sized city in America. For years, Etienne has been represented in the history books with a portrait of another mountain man, Jean Nicolet. But history sleuth D. Robert Carter found two corroborating sketches by Alfred Jacob Miller, who also wrote that Etienne had a "corpus like a porpoise" and that he was "adipose and rotund . . . larding the lean earth" while walking along. (Informed representation by Marilyn Brown.)

Angry Indians made trapping dangerous. But Etienne and his group were open to making peace. When they met to smoke the peace pipe with a group of Shoshones, however, they were not aware that earlier some Hudson Bay explorers had stolen the natives' ponies. Furtively, the revengeful Indians told the trappers the "enchantment" would not work if anyone had "metal objects." So, to be cooperative, the trappers put all of their weapons in a pile on the ground. A few moments later, the Indians drew hidden knives and massacred eight men. Etienne, being rather hefty, was one of the lucky few who got away.

One of the reasons Brigham Young was a great colonizer was that he led with an iron hand. Comparing the Mormons to the ancient Israelites who left Egyptian bondage for freedom in the Promised Land, he organized his emigration companies in the manner of the ancient camps of Israel. When in 1848 Parley P. Pratt and Charles Rich organized for what they felt was faster travel, Brigham roundly scolded them.

Although both men suppressed their hurt, Parley was determined he would make his own settlement in Utah Valley. As soon as he got back to Salt Lake, he and Charles Rich organized a fishing expedition to explore those possibilities at Utah Lake.

About 1,600 pioneers at the Salt Lake settlement managed to live through the winter of 1848. But when the summer's immigration brought their numbers to 4,500, grazing and food grew scarce. As families spread out as far south as "Willow Creek," or Draper, with their livestock, they seemed to do all right—that is until the snow fell. When the cattle began to die, someone suggested there was less snow in Utah Valley. But a committee trek that was sent to discover new grazing lands did not think the cattle could make the difficult trip through the snow.

Desperate for supplies, one party of men—including Oliver B. Huntington, Barney Ward, and Joseph Matthews—went to Utah Valley hoping to trade goods for food. Toward Mapleton, they found an abandoned log cabin whose occupants had probably been frightened off by the Indians. That night, their horses escaped their hobbles, and so they named the area Hobble Creek.

When the Mormons' cattle moved down to Utah Valley, a group of Indians led by Blue Shirt and Roman Nose began killing them for meat. The owners went after them in February 1849 and, to their distress, found the Utes skinning and cooking the cows. In a forced battle at Battle Creek in Pleasant Grove, the robbers were killed, and the militia took the Indian women and children home with them. Though Brigham Young feared the people wanted to settle outside Salt Lake too soon, he agreed they should try to civilize the Indians.

A young Indian warrior, Angatewats, who must have looked very much like those pictured, met the Provo colonists screaming and waving his tomahawk. He tried to stop the families from coming further, but Dimick Huntington, who spoke the Ute language, tried to convince them the settlers meant no harm.

FORT UTAH — VALLEY OF THE GREAT SALT LAKE

But to be safe from the wily natives, the settlers braved the cold and built a fort located on the south bank of the Provo River, where Interstate 15 now crosses that stream. Cautious carpenters put up a central platform to hold the cannon high enough to propel ammunition over the fort wall should the Indians attack. But when on September 1, 1849, militia members George Bean and William Dayton decided to try it out, an unfortunate backfire killed Dayton and took off George's left hand. When Brigham Young visited the fort on September 14, 1849, he asked George "Do you want to live?" George said, "Yes, if I can do any good." "Then you shall live," Young told him. George became a renowned Indian interpreter.

The first fort the settlers built on the Provo River was imagined by the artist Samuel Jepperson. On April 3, 1849, the people began to build this stronghold as rapidly as they could.

When Brigham Young arrived, he chose a new site for the fort, located closer to present-day North Park at Fifth West and Fifth North Streets. Here, the soil was warmer and less alkaline. This painting, also by Samuel Jepperson, depicts the second Fort Utah under construction in the summer and fall of 1850.

Two

THRIVING THROUGH FAMINE AND WAR

Through the first winter, and during harsh years without many crops, the settlers tried fishing in Utah Lake. In the summer of 1849, Parley P. Pratt visited Utah Valley and "saw thousands [of fish] caught by hand." The men with Pratt's party "simply put their hand into the stream, and threw them out as fast as they could pick them up." The fishing industry rose up overnight.

Isabella Horne knit a seine, or fishing net, to be used by the Eutaw Fishing Company. In 1848, Pres. John Smith gave John Forsgren and Pratt, and other members of this company, exclusive rights to fish in Utah Lake. When the grasshoppers came in 1855, the lake became the primary source of food for the colonists.

Even in winter, the settlers took fish from under the ice with nets. At the right with his hands on his hips, George Madsen is shown here with Levi Carpenter (at the far right) and Jake Westphal (third from the left). After the railroad was installed in 1863, they harvested enough fish to send several carloads to New York City every week.

Fisherman George Madsen is shown here in his wedding picture with his wife, Nettie. Madsen followed in his father's footsteps to develop a thriving fishing industry in Provo. The family donated fish to the needy during two depressions, in 1893 and 1930. Always using the seine, it was difficult catching trout when the net was outlawed to protect a dwindling population of fish. His men were sometimes indicted and fined for doing the job they had always done. One employee, Myron C. Newell, spent some time in jail.

The Indians were not happy about the presence of the settlers in their territory hunting and fishing their lake and streams. They goaded the pioneers until a real battle took place. When the Indians seized George Bean's cabin near the Provo River, the settlers made two huge wedges, or V-shaped batteries of wood and approached the natives with gunfire, forcing them to flee or die. One group fled to the south end of Utah Lake, which was where they were slaughtered, and some retreated to the East Mountains. Old Elk and his squaw ran to Rock Canyon, where he was killed. His wife fell from a cliff. The name "Squaw Peak" has been attached to that site ever since.

Squaw Peak rises above Rock Canyon. This winter view suggests how cold the weather might have been in February 1850, when the settlers and Utes fought the battle of Provo River.

From Squaw Peak, these hikers can look out over the entire valley. Walter Pace Cottam took this photograph around 1920.

This elaborate fishing wagon transported fishermen to the lake both for recreation and industry. But fishing was not the only industry to grow when Provo began to expand. Crops were planted from the beginning, although weather, insects, and hoards of Indian horses often destroyed the seedlings before they matured. Below, 10 men are seen threshing grain in a field.

When the Indian problem had been somewhat resolved, it was time to settle in. Enterprising pioneers built this mill in the beautiful American Fork Canyon, using the water power to cut lumber for the construction of homes and shops.

This photograph of an early family mill, built east of Second West Street and north of Bulldog Boulevard, was taken near the turn of the century. It looks as though this Provo miller may have had several wives.

Many temporary buildings were constructed from the crudely milled wood of those who brought it down out of the surrounding hills and used water power to cut it. The photographer who took this picture, George Edward Anderson (1860–1928), often recorded scenes of workers with their animals.

Some of the earliest buildings on Provo's Center Street were constructed of wood. This view, looking west in 1879, shows the north side of Center Street between Second and Third West Streets.

In the following years, as more and more settlers with their wagons and livestock arrived in the valley, brickyards made more permanent structures possible.

In 1899, Center Street was lined with telephone poles and sturdy brick buildings. Some of these structures, such as the building belonging to the Taylor Furniture Company, still stand.

Logs made cozy cabins, but it soon began to be more practical to build with brick. Below, the brick home built by James Clayton was a simple one-story structure, but the double swing was a luxury not many other homes could boast. (Above, C.R. Savage Collection; below, BYU Collection.)

Some of the larger structures were built as hotels. This one, built by Harlow Redfield, eventually became the Bullock Hotel, serving travelers on their way through town on Provo's main thoroughfares, Center Street and Fifth West Street. Later, Academy Avenue, now known as University Avenue, became the central road of the city. The two-story building was situated on the southeast corner of the intersection.

Most of the small adobe houses—sometimes holding several families at the same time—were eventually replaced by larger wooden or brick homes. It looks like the man in the doorway has six wives. Though he proudly had a photograph taken, he knew he would be in danger from the law, so he did not record his name.

This home with two porches, probably built for two polygamous families, shows that new construction in 1880 looked very much like construction today. Yards, trees, and flowers had to wait.

One of Utah's most unfortunate difficulties was the imprisonment of some of its prominent men for the practice of polygamy. Because of their fervent religious beliefs, many—including women and children—found the polygamous lifestyle rewarding. Nevertheless, the practice was appalling to the US government, which made it illegal in 1887 by passing the Edmunds Act.

Federal agents were hired to spy on citizens who appeared to live in more than one home. Or they took the liberty to break into private bedrooms at inopportune times. If the "Feds" were coming, children playing in the street learned codes to warn their parents of danger. Many of these men who practiced polygamy spent years away from their families and months in prison. When released, they were forced to forsake their later wives and children. The irony is that the country's adulterers were going free.

One of Provo's most famous polygamists was Abraham O. Smoot, called to be Provo's first stake president while he was still in Salt Lake City. One of Provo's favorite stories is about how Brigham Young invited Brother Smoot into his office and said, "I am going to call you on a mission. There are three places, all on a par. One is as good as the other. They are: hell, Provo, or Texas." A.O. replied, "I would sooner go to hell than to Provo." Apparently, he did not give a second thought to Texas.

In his Provo home, even Smoot was forced to hide in secret compartments to avoid the federal officers, and even he did not escape going to prison for a time. Like many did in that day, he hired a photographer to take the family's picture standing in the yard.

From simple to ornate, from wood to brick, Victorian architecture gave Provo a distinctive and beautiful beginning that still remains in its pleasant shady avenues and byways. (Above, George Edward Anderson Collection; below, BYU Collection.)

Mormons were not the only religion building beautiful churches and homes. This lovely chapel at Second West and Center Streets was a landmark for the Baptists, who were welcome in Provo with other religious people who found refuge in the West. The Catholics built a beautiful southwestern

place of worship on Second North and Fifth West Streets, a landmark that remained a historic monument until the beginning of the 21st century.

One of the first meetinghouses built by the Mormons was this school building at First North and Fifth West Streets. For a time it was used as both a church and a school.

At the beginning of the 20th century, the seminary was razed; however, an addition was built next to it prior to its demolition. A private academy now occupies this historic building, but it has been renovated several times, holding offices and, at one time, a seafood restaurant.

Before the Church of Jesus Christ of Latter-Day Saints constructed its magnificent tabernacle, which has served many purposes for over a century and a half, it built a meetinghouse on Center Street and what was then Academy Avenue. Looking across the empty field where the NuSkin Building now stands, the old meetinghouse can be seen north of the tabernacle. Notice that this is one of the few photographs showing the original tower on the roof of the tabernacle.

When the original tower on the roof of the tabernacle proved too heavy and began to sink, the congregation removed the tower but left the platform. Eventually, the platform shown here was also removed.

Without question, the kingpin of Provo City and its noble history is its majestic tabernacle. Beset with trials as significant as those of its pioneer builders in the 1860s, after it lost its tower, then its platform, it passed through several other careful retransformations, both in and out. But perhaps the worst tragedy was the one that struck on December 17, 2010, in the middle of the night. A musical group rehearsing for a program the evening of the 16th may have left some electrical equipment still burning. A subsequent investigation reported that a bulb near the ceiling became too hot, caught fire, and began a blaze in the middle of the night.

The destruction of the tabernacle in this terrible fire wounded residents of Provo deeply. "It's like losing a loved one," a bystander lamented. "To replicate that building will take eight to ten million dollars." There was a pause before townspeople said, at the same time, "It's worth it." (Marilyn Brown.)

The indomitable spirit of Provo is much like the miracle of this charred painting of Christ by Harry Anderson rescued by the fire fighters. Most of it may be hurt by the flames, but the image of Christ—the spirit of the work—has been left untouched. (Mark Johnston, *Daily Herald*.)

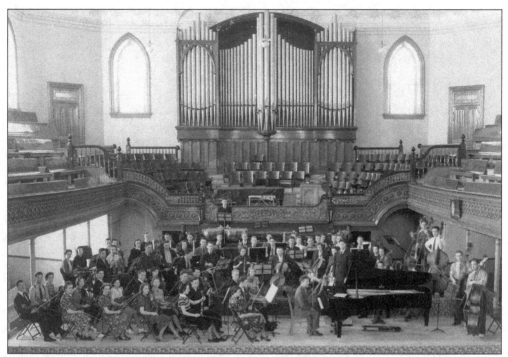

As in years gone by, orchestras and musical productions will return to the tabernacle, as in this group's performance during the 1930s. The acoustics of the building have always been outstanding. In the quiet, audiences can hear the drop of a pin.

When Abraham Smoot's son Reed was the senator for the state, President Taft came to visit Provo's tabernacle. Smoot is in the center, and Taft is at the viewer's right. Unfortunately, at first, the US Senate, still angry with the polygamous Mormons, would not seat Smoot, even though he was not a polygamist. He is famous for telling them, "I would rather be a polygamist that does not polyg than a monogamist who does not monog."

Three

BUILDING INDUSTRY

In addition to the sawmills and brickyards that furnished materials to build homes and shops, a tannery began curing leather in the 1850s to make much-needed shoes. And following the production of leather, because of Utah's agreeable climate for husbandry, it became apparent that one of the best opportunities for clothing people and developing an industry to clothe others lay in wool.

In this image, the men have just shorn their sheep. The wool harvest was so plentiful that, right away, the people in Provo discussed building a woolen mill.

Many of the women, such as Alice Jasperson, above, were hard-working, talented seamstresses who could sew their own clothing and make garments for sale as well. Though this flag may not be wool, it is clear that she was willing, along with many others, to offer her talents and services for the cause of industry.

Once the wool was gathered, it was carefully picked over to remove weeds, rocks, and dead insects. Finally, when the mill was built, there were many looms to accommodate those who had the skill to pull the strands into thread and weave it into cloth.

These photographs show two angles of the woolen mills as they looked when they were finally completed. They were located in the block from First North to Second North and First West to Second West Streets, where the new courthouse now stands. Before the courthouse was built, the smoke stack of the old woolen mills stood until the 1990s.

Perhaps it was the success of the wool industry that was most responsible for Provo's early connection to the world at large. Not only was wool successfully bought and sold locally, as in this city shop, but the Provo product was also shipped all over the United States by rail.

After the last spike joined the railroads in 1869, other connecting railroads became one of the primary occupations of the West, and the Provo workers were just as anxious to build their railroads and rail bridges as everyone else in the country.

Men found steady work building railroads. The railroad station in Provo began with these modest buildings but was rebuilt several times before it became obsolete.

Commerce thrived on railroad shipments of wool, so it was a tragic day for both employees and investors when the mills caught fire in 1918. Though at first, when the smoke rose over the buildings (above), firefighters were hopeful they could save the complex, they were soon overwhelmed, as clearly seen in the photograph below.

The damage to the entire operation was dishearteningly complete. Although the mills had caught on fire once before and profited from rebuilding, the 1918 fire caused irreparable damage. Using the buildings that did not burn, the mills limped on for a while longer, but the fire virtually ended wool production in Provo.

If the fire ended many jobs, the people adjusted. A little-known industry in the area was silk. This float built for the 1897 Pioneer Day parade depicts the silk worm and the mulberry leaves it thrived on to produce the tender cocoons that made strands of silk. When it was discovered that mulberry trees could grow in the Utah climate, this industry became popular all over the state.

Of course, people of Utah still produced livestock, hay, vegetables, and fruits. Their orchards were better established by this time, and residents enjoyed state and local fairs, where they won prizes for their best animals and produce.

At Utah County fairs, like this one held in September 1925, the gardeners displayed the bounteous harvests that sustained their lives. They learned to can and dry food and to keep their bottled fruits and vegetables cool in dirt cellars.

Fairs were not just for food products. The Taylor Furniture Company set up a booth, as did companies such as Knight Coal and Ice and other subsidiary operations of the many companies Jesse Knight built to develop the industrial base in Utah Valley.

The establishment in Olmstead of the Telluride electrical operation in Provo Canyon was one of the most beneficial developments of the 1890s. The water from the river was transported high along the mountainside in giant pipes, and as it fell, power was generated that was transferred through elaborate hydroelectric engineering to furnish electricity for the entire area. The Olmstead complex was named after one of the primary engineers. One of the chief financiers was Lucien L. Nunn. Nunn Park is named for him.

The energy transferred through Provo's Power and Light Company, located between Second and Fifth West and Sixth and Eighth North Streets, gave the city the power to grow and progress in technology and capability.

The Ironton plant in south Provo operated successfully until the last 30 years of the 20th century. It sent metals to Geneva to be used in steel making. The steel industry was important to the entire area.

Sugar beets became one of the area's best industries. Many jobs were created by this sugar mill in Lehi, situated on a millpond near Utah Lake about 20 miles north of Provo.

By 1900, Provo had developed more sophisticated retail markets. The old downtown cattle sales, such as this one, began to be replaced by meat packaging transferred by rail. Businesses, such as Hedquist Drug in the background, began to compete with those from Salt Lake City. Below, like many of the successful businesses on Center Street, Alexander Hedquist had a photographer record the inside of his shop.

Druggists, dentists, and vendors of paint and glass—all of these industries existed together on Center Street. This building still stands in Provo today, continuing to display its beautiful arched windows; its date, 1890; and its name, Excelsior.

Heindselman's also still exists today, and the original family still owns the business. The first proprietor began as an optometrist but expanded into diamonds and stationery and ran the Columbia Music Company. In the 20th century, Erma Dee Heindselman offered instructions on needlework, knitting, and other crafts. At the publication of this book, she is 104 years old and still knits a sweater every week!

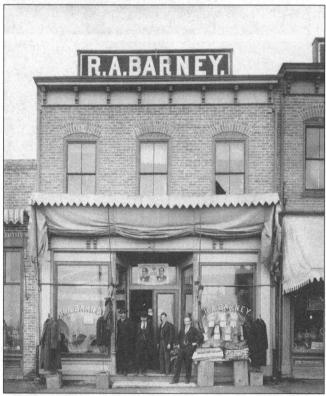

Hardware and men's apparel became successful businesses in Provo. Most of these buildings are still standing, a testimony to the skill of the builders in early Provo history.

Boorey and Milliman was a popular men's clothing store. Most of these businesses were photographed both inside and outside the store by Thomas Christian Larson (1880–1957) or by his son O. Blaine Larson (1906–1986). Some of the photographs, such as this one, show the Larsons' exceptional skill as photographers.

The first "trading and purchasing co-op" was instituted in Provo by two enterprising merchants, Samuel Jones, who had sold peas to the soldiers at Camp Floyd, and David John. Enthusiastically approved by President Smoot, subscriptions for the business soon reached $17,500, and by January 5, 1869, the Provo Co-operative Institution was built at the northeast corner of Center Street and University Avenue, where the Knight Building stands today. Although the Provo Co-op folded in the Panic of 1893, Salt Lake City's Zion's Cooperative Mercantile Institution (ZCMI), which copied Provo, remained in business until the beginning of the 21st century.

This warehouse for the ZCMI, razed long ago, was located on University Avenue at Sixth South Street.

Women, as well as men, must be credited for industry and innovation. They not only owned and operated their own businesses, such as this millinery shop, but they also stood behind their husbands or fathers. This lovely portrait of Anne Hedquist, whose family owned Hedquist Drugs, was taken by another innovative businessman, the successful photographer George Edward Anderson (1860–1928).

This early photograph is rumored to have been taken by the photographer George Edward Anderson of his own family. Though there is no record of exactly who these people are, the facial expressions and the tender bond apparent in the images have made it the favored icon for Provo's online digital archives in the BYU Library.

George Anderson may be the most talented photographer of early Utah Valley history. Many of the best photographs in this book were taken by him. But like every other businessman, building his career was not always easy. He started out taking pictures traveling around using a flimsy tent.

Apparently, a violent storm proved that George Anderson's tent might not have been the best idea. There is no information about the discouraged man in the chair. He may be George's son, feeling disillusionment enough to forsake photography, for there is no record that the business continued in the family.

One of George Anderson's most copied photographs is this scene of a mother and her daughters in prayer. It has been mass produced and found hanging in simple or ornate Victorian frames in many homes of the West.

Four

COMMUNITY SERVICES

The people of Provo were not apathetic about what happened in their community, the quality of education they wanted for their children, or the consequences of national and local issues that impacted their lives. They established responsible government and institutions of higher learning. They were always ready to assemble and let their leaders know how they felt, as in this election rally against Frank Cannon during the depression of the 1890s.

Attention to good government, both federal and local, has always been a priority to Utahns. Because their first government was a theocracy under the leadership of Brigham Young, their "tax" was tithing, usually paid in kind—10 percent of crops, produce, or animals. This representation of the first Provo tithing office is by early painter Samuel Jepperson.

When local, state, and federal taxes began to support the necessary government buildings, the people of Provo built their first auspicious courthouse on the southwest corner of Center Street and First East Street. To the right in the background, the tabernacle is barely visible.

Provo's first large post office is gone now, but this photograph shows its relationship to the intersection of University Avenue and Center Street. The image may have been taken from the roof of the new City and County Building. The lower photograph looks east on Center Street, showing the post office with the City and County Building behind it. To the left of the post office, the tower of the old fire station is visible.

The outstanding Provo City and County Building, with its classic architecture, has long represented Provo's love for beauty and elegance. It still stands as a monument to the sacrifices of thousands of people who desired their city to reflect style and grace. A careful look at the right of the above photograph shows the position of the sheriff's residence. The jail sits behind it, captured at left by an unknown photographer. The darkness in the photograph certainly symbolizes the use of the building.

The fire station, situated on Center Street between the old redbrick courthouse and the post office, no longer stands. Several fire stations now serve the city of Provo. At the extreme right of this image, the tower of the old tabernacle rises above the trees.

Provo's early hospital was the Utah County Infirmary, located on the Springville Road near old Ironton, which is where the juvenile detention center now stands.

When Provo was designated as the home of the state insane asylum, the building was placed on the edge of the city, located far east on Center Street and against the Wasatch Range. It presented some rather interesting architectural transformations from its almost frightening Victorian presence to its more modern face in the late 1900s. It has since undergone still further changes, as has the treatment of mental illness during the last 50 years.

Public access to books was a priority with Provo taxpayers. With the help of Carnegie funds, they built this modest library, which was very soon too small. It was replaced on the same site by the structure pictured below on the northwest corner of First East and Center Streets. In the late 1970s, the library was housed in a building built west of the city offices, now home to the Covey Center for the Arts. At the beginning of the 21st century, it was rebuilt behind the old BYU Academy.

Public schools in Utah have always been very important. Beginning with a tent and a log cabin in Fort Utah, Provo citizens built the Timpanogos School, the Maeser School, and many others. They have redone the Timpanogos School, and the Maeser has now been made into senior housing.

Even the Provo High School on Third West Street, between Center Street and First South Street, became inadequate for the growing number of students. Torn down in the 1960s, it was replaced by the current Provo High School, completed in 1956. The new building has seen other additions but still stands two blocks east of the Utah Regional Medical Center.

This is the building called the "seminary." It was originally built in the 1850s to be a home for George A. Smith. However, the modest leader suggested it was more than he needed, and the town should use it for a school and a community building. It served as a school, the Third Ward meetinghouse, a courthouse, a jail, and a meeting place for government officials.

These men, educators for the First and Second Ward Schools and other private schools at the time, charged a nominal tuition for their services. If parents were lax, Brigham Young scolded them severely: "Men able to ride in their carriages, and not able, or unwilling to pay their children's tuition . . . I know such persons are weak and feeble, but the disease is in the brain and heart. . . . Send your children to school!" Like today, education was sometimes an uphill battle. "The little brats were determined on having a spree," school principal Warren Dusenberry wrote.

When the First Ward Building, on Second East Street between Second and Third South Streets, proved inadequate, the Dusenberrys rented Cluff Hall for $50 a month, then the Kinsey Building, and as enrollment increased, finally the Lewis Building on Third West Street and Center Street, built and owned by Brigham Young. It is the last building on the left in this 1879 photograph.

Brigham Young considered education so vital that he sent Daniel Wells to adopt the "Dusenberry Academy" as the Timpanogos Branch of Salt Lake City's University of Deseret. In 1875, George Q. Cannon and Brigham Young worked on establishing the Brigham Young Academy, and Warren Dusenberry suggested Karl G. Maeser, of the Twentieth Ward Institute, as principal. He was appointed on April 6, 1876.

The Lewis Building began to burst with eager students and faculty as the honored Karl G. Maeser continued to build the reputable BYU Academy. Instructed by Brigham Young to teach mathematics, science, and even the arts with the spirit of God, Maeser relied on the circumspect values of the community to develop honorable citizens.

Brigham Young University Lee Library University Archives; UAP 2

The truth that the LDS Church's saints tried hard to be saints becomes a theme of their dramas, literature, and music, such as in this musical, *The Order Is Love*, by Carol Lynn Pearson. The plot revolves around the failure of the United Order. Considering the reality of conflicting human needs and desires, it is not surprising that the United Order—and "sainthood"—is often destined to have a difficult time.

Karl G. Maeser was teaching at the Lewis Building when on January 27, 1884, it burned down. When a student said, "Oh, Brother Maeser, the academy has burned," Maeser answered, "No such thing, it's only the building." The school met in a bank, a business building, the old ZCMI warehouse, and the old tabernacle until the church and city were able to secure the property on Academy Avenue—now University Avenue—and build the beautiful Victorian structure, completed in 1891. Separating from the university in Salt Lake, it was incorporated on July 18, 1896. As the building grew older, it was used for art and education classes and was then threatened with destruction. Some citizens, led by Shirley and Monroe Paxman, were concerned about its preservation, hoping in the 1970s to use it for a library. However, the city built another library, which lasted only a few years and was finally refurbished to house the Covey Center for the Arts. The city fathers, finally realizing that the library should be built on Academy Square, have re-stabilized and restored the magnificent structure at great cost, putting the new library where it should have gone years ago. The prodigious cost will be forgotten, but the beautiful Academy Building never will.

The above class of BYU graduates on May 26, 1904, celebrated their commencement with a photograph taken on the south lawn of the new tabernacle. Below, on June 2, 1916, they completed their ceremony in the auditorium of College Hall, which was built behind the Academy Building and eventually razed for the construction of the Provo Library.

B.Y.U. Graduates   1915-'16   June 2nd 1916

The school was destined for another century of exciting development, as land was purchased on the brow of the hill northeast of the Academy Building. It was here that greater expansion would be possible. On October 16, 1909, the president of the Church of Jesus Christ of Latter-Day Saints, Joseph F. Smith, with the white beard, conducted an exciting ceremony in which the cornerstone of the new Maeser Building was laid.

By 1929, the Maeser Building, dedicated in 1911, was accompanied by the Heber J. Grant Library to the far right and the one-story Mechanic Arts Building, shown above, which became the Brimhall Building in 1935 with the addition of two stories. BYU maintained the farmlands that waited for the university's further expansion.

This 1974 view of the university is spectacular. By this time, the university was accommodating 25,000 students in 300 buildings, with a staff of more than 3,000.

From arts to athletics, BYU rose to the top. In 1896, its first football team, organized by Pres. Benjamin Cluff Jr., beat the University of Utah 12-0!

Academics have always been a top priority. From left to right, Donald K. Nelson, the director of libraries; Roy E. Christensen, donor and president of Beverly Enterprises; and Robert K. Thomas, the vice-president of academics in 1969, examine a $143,000 gift of rare Victorian books donated to the BYU Library. It is the dedication and generosity of the archivists in the L. Tom Perry Special Collections of the BYU Library that has made possible most of the photographs in this book.

Five

ENRICHING LIVES

As people become educated and prosperous, they begin to wish not only to survive but also to add accomplishment, beauty, and grace to their lives. The architecture of this outstanding home built in Provo is a testimony to the dreams of Julius Hannberg, who yearned to remember the castles along the Rhine in his homeland. Investors later razed it to make room for an apartment complex.

Jesse Knight, one of the sons of Joseph Smith's friend Newell Knight of the early church, was not only a successful miner in Eureka but also a developer of several businesses that furnished many jobs for the community. His beautiful home on Center Street was long ago purchased by the Berg Mortuary and stands today as an exceptional structure of architectural grace. His descendants still give generously to philanthropic causes.

The Mangum residence, on the northwest corner of Fourth East and Center Streets, was built by Jesse Knight as a wedding present for his daughter when she married Lester Mangum.

The McDonald house, on First North Street between Third and Fourth East Streets, was another of the most beautiful homes in Provo. The interior of the new Roberts Hotel hints at the luxury characteristic of Provo's best buildings. The Roberts Hotel and the Catholic church were both victims of the wreckers' ball at the beginning of the 21st century.

Businesses, as they became more prosperous, developed newer facilities. Modern architecture took its place beside the old on Center Street. Although Woolworth thrived next to the Excelsior Building, it soon built its own structure directly across the street on the lot where the NuSkin Building now stands.

Provo's old railroad station was located near University Avenue and Sixth South Street. There was a bitter controversy over where to build the new station. Businessman Thomas N. Taylor led the effort to purchase the site at Sixth South and Third West Streets without the approval of Jesse Knight, who wanted the station to be built to the east. An election in July 1909 narrowly confirmed Taylor's choice. Though still in Taylor's location, the station has been rebuilt as a small depot for passenger trains.

PROVO CITY, UTAH

In the early 1900s, as people could afford more leisure time, they built a newfangled streetcar up Center Street, which turned north at University Avenue. The Orem Station was where NuSkin now stands. The photograph below shows the roundhouse, where cars were stored and repaired.

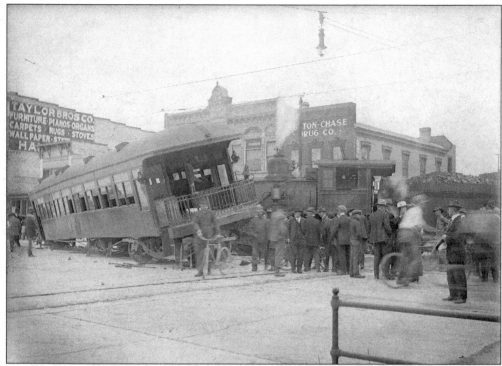

All that was modern was not easy. A photographer, believed to be George Anderson, took excellent photographs of an Orem Inter-Urban train hit broadside by a Heber Creeper. The Taylor Brothers' sign on the upper left indicates the Second West Street–Center Street intersection as the location of the accident.

Though at times a ride on the railroad may have proven risky, still the temptation was great to take the train to the Upper Falls or south to the Castilla Springs. Shown below, "old folks," who made ceremonious events of their weekend outings, traveled to the springs, where natural hot waters soothed their bones.

Sometimes, when modern conveniences just seem to cause more distress, one wants to return to the old methods of transportation.

Camping was sometimes a joyful distraction from a busy life, or sometimes a necessity. When the US Army forced the people of Salt Lake City to move to Provo, many families set up tents in Provo's spare lots. Provo people were not always happy with the intruders, as their cattle had not been trained to use proper facilities.

But camping and picnicking have always been popular, and though campers are now using more sophisticated vehicles for their excursions, the yearning still remains to eat outside, sleep out under the stars, and enjoy nature.

The outdoor hiking trip on the back of Timpanogos every summer was a tradition until it was obvious that so many feet on the mountain were causing damage. Eugene Roberts, an attractive physical education teacher from BYU, was a legendary leader on those hikes, which were known to attract a female following.

Sundance has always been a popular ski resort. At first named Timp Haven for its location at the back side of Mount Timpanogos, it—and the lodge built by the same name—became many a scene for church parties, outings, and even corporate rendezvous. When Robert Redford bought the site in the mid-1900s, it became the birthplace of a now world-famous film festival.

Another recreational spot in Provo Canyon is the beautiful Bridal Veil Falls. In spite of the danger in building at the top of the falls—one man was killed—the restaurant and dancing facilities and the tram ride up to it furnished an exciting and romantic evening for many BYU social clubs and corporate events. After a fire, owner David Grow was forced to take the tram down.

In the late 19th century, the old Provo City Railroad took people out to Utah Lake during the summer.

The *Florence* is shown here with the engine that transported it to Utah Lake. A pleasure boat that many people enjoyed on the lake, it was finally sold and moved to the Great Salt Lake. To the right, one can see a foundry located at Fifth West and Center Streets.

Utah Lake has long been a prime recreational area. The former state park headquarters at the lake and the tower overlooking it are reminders of an earlier time. Below, cement is being poured to form the old ice skating rink, which has now been removed.

Further north on the lake, the popular Geneva Resort furnished cabins, pontoons, and rowboats for many Provo citizens seeking to get away from a long week of hard work.

In the late 1800s, the lake hosted not only leisurely pleasure boats but also fiercely competitive rowing races and regattas. This is a studio portrait of the lightweight crew of the Provo Boat Club. It was one of the winning teams in 1890. (George Edward Anderson Collection.)

When it was too cold for boating, people enjoyed sleigh rides. In the spring, they flocked to the golf course in south Provo, which has furnished many a golfer a sunny day at the foot of the Wasatch Mountains.

As soon as pleasure-seekers finished their outdoor activities, they had an opportunity to come into town and enjoy theaters and restaurants. The movie theater at the left with the white arch was very popular for years, but after the bats and mice infested it, the building had to be taken down. This photograph shows the fountain that stood from 1917 to 1931 in the middle of the intersection at University Avenue and Center Street. The fountain was removed because of increased automobile traffic.

Though gone now, an early opera house built on First West Street, between Center Street and First North Street, furnished a place for large meetings, dramas, and concerts. It was later used as a National Guard armory and a hall where students could play basketball.

In addition to attending the movie theater and dramatic productions, the community also thrived on gathering for special events, such as this motorcade on University Avenue, or parades, like this procession of Boy Scout troops on May Day, 1925.

One of Provo's most prominent events was President Taft's visit on Pioneer Day, July 24, 1914. Hundreds of people gathered at the railroad station to greet him. It was a treat for the citizens and their children to see the president and to know he cared enough about Utah to honor their courageous pioneers.

This gathering took place in the vacant lot across the street from the Taylor buildings, which still stand. The event looks like a sale or a horse show. The ownership of beautiful animals was still important long into the 20th century.

The Ringling Bros. Circus made many welcome visits to Provo, even in the earliest years of its existence—when transportation was by horse, carriage, or bicycles.

This 1912 image of the circus parade shows that it took place in the popular intersection of University Avenue and Center Street. The tabernacle is visible behind it, still bearing its heavy tower, which was eventually removed.

With spring weather, reunions, homecomings, and other special occasions gave citizens a cause to celebrate together. To honor their dead on Memorial Day, those who lost loved ones have always decorated the graves in the beautiful Provo Cemetery, which is now short a few trees from a micro-windburst. At right, many war widows and other single women, like Luell Chase and her daughter, honored the memory of both their husband and father.

Homecoming parades and football games are always spectacular displays of student talent, athletic prowess, and musical aptitude. This parade took place in 1934 during the Depression, which was around the same time the Provo band played in the same intersection.

For many years, the people of the city held special ceremonies to honor their veterans. For the World War I veterans who had returned home, they assembled in front of the courthouse on Center Street to give them the respect and praise they deserved.

Keeping history alive, the veterans of Provo's early Indian wars continued to hold eventful reunions in tourist destinations all over the state. At this one in Provo, they gathered north of the tabernacle.

The veterans also enjoyed their own martial band, a "drum and fife" organization. Below, a full orchestra helped celebrate the 77th birthday of Provo, which was held in the Provo Tabernacle on March 12, 1926.

DAUGHTERS AND PIONEERS CELEBRATE PROVO'S 77 BIRTHDAY MARCH 12-1926. PROVO. UTAH. C.E.A PHOTO.

This is the August 2, 1927, Veteran Commander Band on their sixth annual encampment at Heber, Utah. The members of these musical organizations played for special events all over the valley, staying with their ensemble until all of them were senior citizens.

Veterans, their wives, and senior citizen groups also enjoyed the culinary arts. This picnic took place at Castilla Springs on June 16, 1905.

This Indian War veterans' reunion allows a rare glimpse of the beauty of the old Salt Air Resort in Salt Lake City before it was destroyed by fire. These celebrations always included a band and a remarkable presence of Indians—or citizens dressed as Indians—as a reminder that reconciliation between the two cultures has been accomplished.

The harbinger of all of these events was usually the *Daily Herald*, serving the people with printed news for over 130 years. The offices changed locations several times, but the paper's responsibility to make accurate reports never wavered.

At times of disaster, such as the explosion at Schofield Mine, reporters from the *Daily Herald* were always there to bring the historic details to the Provo readers.

The history of authors, publishers, and printers in Provo is not an insignificant one. This beautiful renaissance-worthy photograph of an employee in the Hiller Book bindery reminds people that the printed word has been the singular reason why information is known of war, politics, and lives that have come before those of today. Now, words combined with images, such as those in this book, are important records of history for future generations.

Six

Up-to-Date City

There are only a few things that don't alter much over time, and this scene on the Provo River could just as well take place now as in the 1950s.

Since the above historic photograph was taken in 1946, Provo's University Avenue skyline has recently added two huge new buildings, Wells Fargo and a new Zions Bank. (Below, Marilyn Brown.)

In 2010, the yard north of the tabernacle that once held an early meetinghouse is now a historic spot marked by an informative monument. (Marilyn Brown.)

And just west of the tabernacle is the NuSkin Building with its beautiful sculpture by Gary Price, which symbolizes the hope for unity in the world. (Valerie Holladay.)

This view of Provo's Center Street clearly reveals the location of the old woolen mills in the distance. The courthouse now occupies the block between First and Second North Streets.

Except for the addition of smart black awnings, the old drugstore at First West and Center Streets, now owned by NuSkin, looks very much the same. Behind it stands the Provo Marriott Hotel, which is part of the expansion now taking place—a project that will furnish Provo with a first-class conference center for national corporate meetings and conventions. (Marilyn Brown.)

The Utah Valley Conference Center, now in the Marriott Hotel, is at this moment in 2010 in the midst of construction. The buildings in the picture below, showing the old dance hall, have been razed for the project, but the Continental Mall, the remodeled old Taylor Furniture Buildings at the left, will be maintained for historic preservation.

This rare photograph, taken in 1902 by an unknown photographer, shows the old tabernacle and the back of the new tabernacle. These streets look very different now.

The new Health and Justice Building, shown above, now stands diagonally across the street east of the tabernacle. It is on the spot that was once occupied by the mansion on the extreme right in the photograph above. (Valerie Holladay.)

This photograph was taken on the southwest corner of one of Provo's historic intersections, First South Street and University Avenue. The stretch of lawn seen above is now the site of the huge Utah County Administration Building, complete with a five-story indoor parking lot. From behind the complex, this view was taken on First South Street.

The City Center, now on the south side of Center Street between Third and Fourth West Streets, houses the City Government Offices. (Marilyn Brown.)

West of the city complex is the old library, now remodeled as the new Covey Center for the Arts, with major financial support by Stephen Covey, nationally acclaimed author of *The Seven Habits of Highly Effective People*. His wife, Sandra, wanted the city to have a beautiful place to host a show or put up art. The generosity of the Coveys has added much class to the culture of the city. (Marilyn Brown.)

The bandstand of the 1930s may be gone from Pioneer Park, but in this square, between Fifth and Sixth West and First South and Center Streets, vendors now set up their colorful tents and sell their produce and crafts every Saturday morning from spring to fall for the farmers' market. (Below, Marilyn Brown.)

Visitors to the farmers' market may see the towering monument that has been erected to honor the pioneers who carved this city out of the wilderness. (Marilyn Brown.)

Up the street on Fifth West and Fifth North Streets, the historic Provo Pioneer Museum gives tourists and history buffs a chance to visit relics from Provo's historic past—some of the clothing made by the woolen mills, military regalia, and old documents and photographs. (Marilyn Brown.)

In back of the museum is Provo's outdoor community swimming pool and playground, a favorite of children and adults alike. On the mountain on the left, BYU's signature advertisement, its huge Y, can be seen on this clear day. The buildings in back of this park are the senior citizens' Eldred Center and the youth center.

This well-preserved Fifth West Street mansion, now used for a reception center, was gifted by its owner to the city to be used as a library for the west side. However, because other plans were being made for the library, the mayor, Verl G. Dixon, bought the gift, setting his own low price at $5,000, and used it for his home. (Marilyn Brown.)

In addition to the preservation of Provo's beautiful mansions, some of the churches have remained intact. This beautiful old church, the Provo First Ward Chapel, still stands on Second South and Second East Streets. Today, the architecture remains as traditional as it was in these photographs, taken in 1928.

Because the city is built between a range of large mountains and a lake, it expanded southward in order to grow its commercial base. With city founders reluctant to build a mall in the city, Provo lost much of its business to the University Mall in Orem, which hastened the construction of the first-rate Provo Towne Center.

Other companies were also attracted to the open spaces at both the southern end of University Avenue and the northern end at the Riverwoods Mall. Complexes of commercial buildings in Provo have exploded in both places. Novell, below, one of Provo's most important industries, has become internationally acclaimed. (Both, Valerie Holladay.)

Perhaps the most unique feature of Provo has always been the student population. While Provo has developed commerce, it will still always remain a university town. Even though the Provo Technical College has now been transformed into the Utah Valley University, it must not be forgotten that it had its humble beginnings in Provo. Educating students in vital fields, such as auto and farm mechanics, nursing, driver education, electronics, and business, the college stayed in Provo until it became this sprawling presence in the 1960s. Eventually, it found an impressive home in Orem.

Students, learning hands-on skills that support the community, dismantle a sub-station framework.

It would be interesting to ask the hundreds and thousands of students who have passed through training at Provo Tech or BYU what they remember most about their experiences here. Working on an old bomber, donated in 1943 to the mechanics classes, might have made the awareness of the world wars unforgettable.

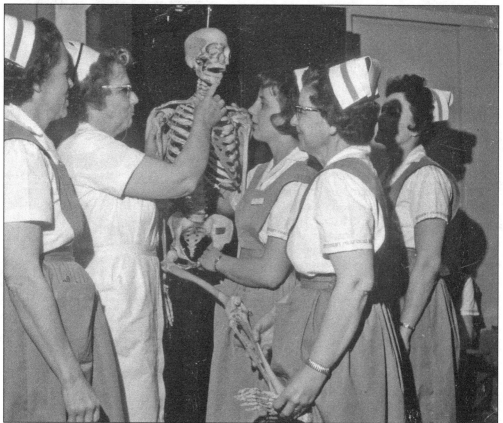

Unlocking their futures with the "skeleton key" may have been one of the most memorable moments for the many students who went through the practical nursing program on Provo Tech's campus.

What cannot be denied is that the thousands of students who have passed through both colleges will never forget their university years in the quaint town of Provo. If they do not remember their classes, their grades, or their teachers, at least they may not forget the famous Stan's Diner, located on Ninth East Street, or Heaps o' Pizza.

Or they will remember the talented International Folk Dancers, shown here, dancing on their tour to Belgium in 1968.

Dramas, pageants, parades, winning ball games, old romances, or special dates with people almost forgotten may spark memories. Perhaps everyone has gone full circle. This *Legend of Timpanogos* production was an attempt in 1937 to remember the Indians. It could be that participation in the arts—even in browsing through artistic old photographs such as these—may be the best way to remember the past.

How can anyone forget Janie Thompson and her contagious enthusiasm for the Program Bureau, Pres. Ernest Wilkinson's energetic handshake, or the thousands of others too numerous to mention who influenced those living in Provo today? Because Provo has been fortunate enough to avoid some of the conflicts and trials that have beset other cities in the country, it exemplifies stress-free living in the best sense.

Perhaps one of the most symbolic activities of any community is the razing and building that citizens perform to create new structures where people can continue to grow and develop responsibilities for the future. This September 1, 1969, photograph of Pres. Hugh B. Brown, Joseph Fielding Smith, and Gordon B. Hinckley breaking the ground for the Provo Temple is a memorable image of how Provo is destined to join the larger world community in its quest for eternal values, beauty, human strength of character, and honor.

Always a beacon of historical progress, responsible government, and joyful learning experiences, this city will forever sparkle in the memory like a jewel—even in times of darkness. The future is in our hands.

Visit us at
arcadiapublishing.com

CPSIA information can be obtained
at www.ICGtesting.com
Printed in the USA
LVHW100826151120
671745LV00005B/98

9 781531 656478